Axel Jörn

Pfizer and the Challenges of the Global Pharmaceutical Industry

Anchor Academic Publishing

Jörn, Axel: Pfizer and the Challenges of the Global Pharmaceutical Industry, Hamburg, Anchor Academic Publishing 2016

Buch-ISBN: 978-3-96067-006-3
PDF-eBook-ISBN: 978-3-96067-506-8
Druck/Herstellung: Anchor Academic Publishing, Hamburg, 2016

Bibliografische Information der Deutschen Nationalbibliothek:
Die Deutsche Nationalbibliothek verzeichnet diese Publikation in der Deutschen Nationalbibliografie; detaillierte bibliografische Daten sind im Internet über http://dnb.d-nb.de abrufbar.

Bibliographical Information of the German National Library:
The German National Library lists this publication in the German National Bibliography. Detailed bibliographic data can be found at: http://dnb.d-nb.de

All rights reserved. This publication may not be reproduced, stored in a retrieval system or transmitted, in any form or by any means, electronic, mechanical, photocopying, recording or otherwise, without the prior permission of the publishers.

Das Werk einschließlich aller seiner Teile ist urheberrechtlich geschützt. Jede Verwertung außerhalb der Grenzen des Urheberrechtsgesetzes ist ohne Zustimmung des Verlages unzulässig und strafbar. Dies gilt insbesondere für Vervielfältigungen, Übersetzungen, Mikroverfilmungen und die Einspeicherung und Bearbeitung in elektronischen Systemen.

Die Wiedergabe von Gebrauchsnamen, Handelsnamen, Warenbezeichnungen usw. in diesem Werk berechtigt auch ohne besondere Kennzeichnung nicht zu der Annahme, dass solche Namen im Sinne der Warenzeichen- und Markenschutz-Gesetzgebung als frei zu betrachten wären und daher von jedermann benutzt werden dürften.

Die Informationen in diesem Werk wurden mit Sorgfalt erarbeitet. Dennoch können Fehler nicht vollständig ausgeschlossen werden und die Diplomica Verlag GmbH, die Autoren oder Übersetzer übernehmen keine juristische Verantwortung oder irgendeine Haftung für evtl. verbliebene fehlerhafte Angaben und deren Folgen.

Alle Rechte vorbehalten

© Anchor Academic Publishing, Imprint der Diplomica Verlag GmbH
Hermannstal 119k, 22119 Hamburg
http://www.diplomica-verlag.de, Hamburg 2016
Printed in Germany

Contents

List of figures 6

List of tables 6

List of abbreviations 6

1   Introduction 7
    1.1   Task of Assignment 7
    1.2   Basic information about Pfizer 7

2   The global pharmaceutical industry and its „boundaries" 8
    2.1   Loss of Exclusivity – Increasing Generic Problem 8
    2.2   Regulatory Environment 9
    2.3   Global economic environment 9

3   The overall trends in the pharmaceutical industry 11
    3.1   Growing trend of "personalized medication" 11
    3.2   Growing trend of "Self-Care" 11

4   The profitability/attractiveness of the global pharmaceutical industry 13
    4.1   Bargaining power of buyers 13
    4.2   Bargaining power of the suppliers 16
    4.3   Threats of substitutes products 17
    4.4   Threats of new entrants 18
    4.5   Rivalry among competitors 20
    4.6   Result of five force analyses 23

5   Future profitability/attractiveness in the pharmaceutical industry 24

6   The strategy of Pfizer 25

7   Applied business and marketing strategy in the recent years 26
    7.1   Strategic changes 27
    7.2   Strategic sales, M&A, partnerships and alliances 28

List of references 29

List of internet references 29

List of figures

Figure 1: Pfizer - Recent Losses of Product Exclusivity Impacting Product Revenues 8
Figure 2: Annual average growth rate in health expenditures per capita, 2000 to 2010.......... 10
Figure 3: Sales of organic food world in the years 1999 to 2012 (in billion US dollars) 12
Figure 4: Geographical Breakdown Medicine-Sales launched in the period of 2009-2013. ... 14
Figure 5: Distribution model of the pharmaceutical industry. 15

List of tables

Table 1: Scoring summery of barriers for entering the market for pharmaceuticals. 20
Table 2: Scoring summery of reality among competitors the market for pharmaceuticals. 22
Table 3: Pfizer five force environment and resulting challenges... 23
Table 4: Challenges and Pfizer's resulting strategic objectives... 25

List of abbreviations

RoW	Rest of World
OECD	Organisation for Economic Cooperation and Development
WHO	World health organisation
WTO	World trade organisation
CDV	Cardiovascular diseases
CAM	Complementary and alternative medicine
OTC	Over-the-counter-drugs = prescription-free medicines
M&A	Merger and Acquisitions
IPO	Initial Public Offering

1 Introduction

1.1 Task of Assignment

This Case Study "Pfizer and the Challenges of the Global Pharmaceutical Industry" was created in the first semester marketing module to obtain the „Master of Business Administration" and covers the following topics or answers the following questions:

- Define the global pharmaceutical industry and its „boundaries".
- What overall industry trends can be identified?
- Analyse the profitability/attractiveness of the global pharmaceutical industry by using M.E.Porters´ Five-Forces-Model.
- How will the profitability/attractiveness of the industry change in the future?
- Please explain and evaluate Pfizer´s new strategy.
- What did Pfizer in the recent years to maintain their profitability?

1.2 Basic information about Pfizer

The cousins Charles Pfizer and Charles Erhart founded Pfizer in 1849 in New York City as a manufacturer of fine chemicals. After its discovery of Terramycin (oxytetracycline) in 1950 Pfizer become a research-based pharmaceutical company. During the 1980s and 1990s, Pfizer Corporation growth was sustained by the discovery and marketing of Zoloft, Lipitor, Norvasc, Zithromax, Aricept, Diflucan and Viagra. In order to expand and strengthen its business, Pfizer has made numerous acquisitions, including Warner–Lambert in 2000, Pharmacia in 2003 and Wyeth in 2009. With total revenue of $51.6 billion in 2013[1] and more than 78,000 employees worldwide, Pfizer became one of the world's largest pharmaceutical companies by revenue. The global portfolio of Pfizer includes medicines and vaccines, as well as many of the world's best-known consumer healthcare products.[2] The majority of Pfizers revenues come from the manufacture and sale of biopharmaceutical products. After the loss of exclusivity for several branded products, Pfizer faces a number of industry-specific challenges, which can significantly impact their further results.

---

[1] Rf.: Pfi-Fi Re (2013), page 2
[2] Rf.: Pfi-Fi Re (2013), page 2

2 The global pharmaceutical industry and its „boundaries"

The pharmaceutical industry is highly competitive and highly regulated. As a result, it faces a lot of different challenges in their business environment. Not only Pfizer, but also all big Pharma companies, have to reinvent themselves and change or modify their earlier strategies. The "boundaries" for the pharmaceutical industry cover a wide variety of areas including industry specific factors and also the effects of the challenging economic environment. Below three major boundaries are pictured.

2.1 Loss of Exclusivity – Increasing Generic Problem

The loss or expiration of intellectual property rights and the expiration of licencing rights have a significant adverse effect on the revenues of all affected pharmaceutical companies. After the loss of exclusivity for its "Blockbuster" Lipitor, Pfizer faces multi-sources generic competition in the affected markets. The revenues for Lipitor decline from $9.6 billion in 2011 to $3.9 billion in 2012 and in 2013 down to $2.3 billion.

The following table provides information about certain of our products impacted by losses of exclusivity (LOEs) in 2013 and 2012 (other than Lipitor), showing, by product, the LOE dates, the markets impacted and the revenues associated with those products in those LOE markets:

(MILLIONS OF DOLLARS)			Revenues in Markets Impacted		
Products	LOE Dates	Markets Impacted	Year Ended December 31,		
			2013	2012	2011
Xalatan and Xalacom	January 2012	Majority of European markets	$ 161	$ 275	$ 509
Aricept	February and April 2012	Majority of European markets	47	139	347
Geodon	March 2012	U.S.	84	214	859
Revatio tablet	September 2012	U.S.	67	312	312
Detrol IR and Detrol LA	September 2012	Majority of European markets	53	119	157
Lyrica	February 2013	Canada	101	206	185
Viagra	June 2013	Majority of European markets	265	370	400

Figure 1: Pfizer - Recent Losses of Product Exclusivity Impacting Product Revenues[3]

The discovery of a new product costs the pharmaceutical companies many years and millions of dollars with no guarantee for a successful approval from the responsible authorities. The companies are able to take advantage of their hard work and investments while their patents are in effect, but as soon as the patents for the "Blockbuster" expire, the generic drug makers

---

[3] Rf.: Pfi-Fi Re (2013), page 4

are able to produce lower cost and in most cases very effective alternatives, and therefore undercut the margins of the big Pharma companies within a very short time.

2.2 Regulatory Environment

Governments, managed care organizations and other payer groups try to reduce the spending on healthcare through a variety of means.

Governments try to ensure through different regulatory changes, like the Patient Protection and Affordable Care Act (enacted in U.S in March 2010), that the expected benefits are aligned with the costs for the insurance, products and services.[4] Through implemented price controls and demanding cuts (directly or by rebate actions) they continue to seek increasing discounts on the pharmaceutical products.[5]

Animal Right groups and many other groups often not only have the monetary resources but also the political connection that can make it very difficult for Pharma companies to operate to their full potential in many countries and markets.

Health insurers and benefit plans continue to limit access to certain branded medicine by imposing formulary restrictions in favor of the increased use of generics.[6] All these regulations will have current and long-term impacts on the pharmaceutical industry.

2.3 Global economic environment

The effects of the global economic environment have an impact on the pharmaceutical industry, not only in the developed markets (U.S., Europe), but also in a number of emerging markets. Patients, experiencing the effects of the challenging economic environment, including high unemployment levels and increase costs in co-payments, sometimes switch to generic products, delay treatments, skip doses or use less effective treatments to reduce their costs.
In the U.S. the challenging economic conditions also have increased the number of patients in the Medicaid program, under which sales of pharmaceuticals are subject to substantial rebates and, in many states, to formulary restrictions limiting access to brand-name drugs. In the most European countries there is compulsory health insurance supported by the state and is acces-

---

[4] Rf.: Pfi-Fi Re (2013), page 5
[5] Rf.: Pfi-Fi Re (2013), page 6
[6] Rf.: Baines (2010), Page 11-12

sible for the whole population. Based on this, the national health systems are the basic principal payer for medicines in Europe.

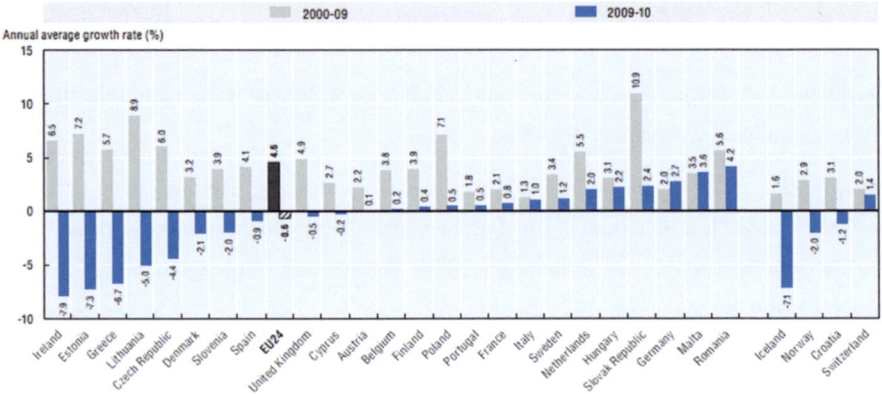

Figure 2: Annual average growth rate in health expenditures per capita, 2000 to 2010[7]

Considering the increasing health care spending and tight national budgets, the pharmaceutical industry continue to experiencing price pressure through government-mandated reductions in prices for certain biopharmaceutical products and government-imposed access restrictions in certain countries. Furthermore, some government agencies and third-party payers use health technology assessments in ways that, at times, lead to lower prices for and restricted access to new medicines.[8]

---

[7] Rf.: OECD 2012, page 121
[8] Rf.: Pfi-Fi Re (2013), page 7

3 The overall trends in the pharmaceutical industry

There are several trends impacting the pharma industry, nevertheless the following section introduces only two trends who have mostly impacted the pharma industry in the last years. The five force analysis of this assignment explains and refers to additional trends.

3.1 Growing trend of "personalized medication"

Blockbuster drugs, being money-spinners, have dominated the pharmaceutical industry. Problems such as expensive large-scale clinical trials, shortened life expectancy of the drug, competition from generic drugs and safety issues are steering the industry towards personalized medication. The "new sciences" like biotechnology, genetics, pharmacogenomics and proteomics will allow to prescribe medication based on the patient`s genotype, maximizing the effectiveness and minimizing side effects.[9] The development processes of this "personalized medication" have little to do with the traditional R&D of the large pharmaceutical firms. Universities and smaller biotechnology firms increasingly rank higher in innovations than the large pharmaceutical firms.

3.2 Growing trend of "Self-Care"

A growing trend towards increasing self-responsibility in health can be observed. More and more people are making healthy choices such as getting regular exercise, eating a balanced diet, refraining from smoking and managing stress. Making organic lifestyle choices is part of this growing trend. Many supermarkets, health food stores, farmer markets, consumer supported agriculture programs and host of other organizations help to make organic product available to the consumer. According to reports from a number of Organic Growers groups, this sector is growing faster than other.[10]

---

[9] Rf.: Frost (2006)
[10] Rf.: OrgLiCh (2014)

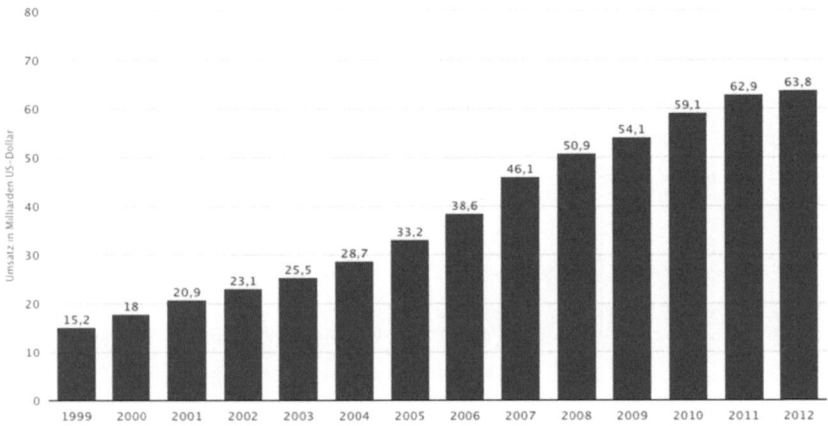

Figure 3: Sales of organic food world in the years 1999 to 2012 (in billion US dollars)[11]

Healthcare is also moving towards a precision model of personal care. Self-care is a primary form of care for various chronic diseases namely diabetes, blood pressure, cardiovascular and others. It is referred to as an action that contributes in maintaining personal health with the use of various self-monitoring devices. Self-care medical devices play a major role in providing that ultimately help for patients or individuals to manage episodic acute and chronic illnesses. Increasing patient population coupled with rising awareness of lifestyle disorders and rapid technological developments in medical devices have accentuated the growth of the self-care medical devices market globally.[12]

---

[11] Rf.: Statista (2014)
[12] Rf.: PRNewswire, ALBANY

4 The profitability/attractiveness of the global pharmaceutical industry

The profitability and attractiveness is constrained to the competition in the market. To determine the computational environment one must not just analyse the established industry rivals. Moreover the four other competitive forces: customers, suppliers, potential entrants, and substitute products must be considered. "The extended rivalry that results from all five forces defines an industry's structure and shapes the nature of competitive interaction within an industry."[13] The relevant industry for this investigation is defined by the 2014 Pfizer medicine product portfolio. The Wellness and other products are not part of this investigation. The scope of the competition is the overall global with a major focus on Pfizer US core market.

4.1 Bargaining power of buyers

The power of the buyers (patient, doctors and pharmacies) is mainly linked to the demand and their price sensitivity. In general the pharmaceutical industry faces an increasing demand and their buyers are price sensitive in the market for generics and not price sensitive in the market of patent protected medicines, as these have no alternatives. The already mentioned and the following trends and facts will prove that.

Demographical change (ageing population): "On average across OECD countries, the share of the population aged over 65 years has increased from less than 9% in 1960 to 15% in 2010 and is expected to nearly double in the next four decades to reach 27% in 2050"[14] An increasing number of older people courses soring need for health care and medication.

Globalisation: A major component of the globalisation is the liberalization of international trade and consequently the globalization of health risks. These risks include tobacco, alcohol, global epidemics of non-communicable diseases and trade in health services. "The World Health Organization (WHO) estimates that the death toll from tobacco abuse alone will reach 10 million a year over the next two decades. Up to 70% of these deaths, caused by lung cancer, cardiovascular diseases (CVDs), lung diseases, diabetes and many other tobacco-related

---

[13] Rf.: Porter (2008), page 79
[14] Rf.: OPEG (2013), page 170

ailments, will occur in developing countries"[15] The impact of alcohol consumption is complex. Moreover we can state that there is a strong constraint between alcohol consumption and liver cirrhosis, some cancers, and most causes of injuries and violence. According to the WHO non communicable diseases (cancers, diabetes, obesity and CVD) will make two-thirds of global disease burden in 2012 climbing from 40% in 2014.

Another aspect is the Globalization of trade. The World Trade Organisation (WTO) manifested an agreement on Intellectual Property Rights, which extends patent protection on new drugs for a minimum period of 20 years. As a result of high prices, this threatens to limit and undermine access to new medicines, especially in the developing world. In this sense, the extension of patent protection can be seen as exacerbating health risks. "Trade and movement of infected cattle and poultry across national borders may also have contributed to recent outbreaks of mad cow disease in the northern hemisphere and avian influenza in Asia."[16] Long haul flights or air travel in general facilitates the spread of contagious diseases. A person in the early stages of an infectious disease can be function as a vector for that disease to aiding its spread into vulnerable and non-immune populations. All these globalisation trends are very strong indicators for a higher demand for pharmaceuticals in the future.

Emerging markets: "Leading emerging countries will account for 28% of the global spending for pharmaceuticals in 2015 compared to 12% in 2005."[17] "In 2013 the Brazilian and Chinese markets grew by 17% and 14%"[18]. In general there is a massive growing potential as only 9% of new medicine launched between 2009 and 2013 is occupied by the Rest of World (RoW) markets. The graphic below pictures the current distribution and gives evidence of the future market development direction.

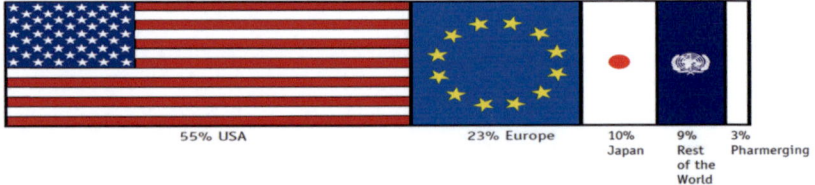

Figure 4: Geographical Breakdown Medicine-Sales launched in the period of 2009-2013.

---

[15] Rf.: USNLM (2014)
[16] Rf.: USNLM (2014)
[17] ifpma (2012), page 5
[18] efpin (2014), page 4

The fact that the pharmaceutical market is mushrooming and the hunger in the developing countries for pharmaceutical products is going to grow more in the coming years, are proving the future attractiveness of the market.

Liberalising distribution channels: The distribution channels can be best described with the following picture. The changing business areas in the current model are highlighted in red.

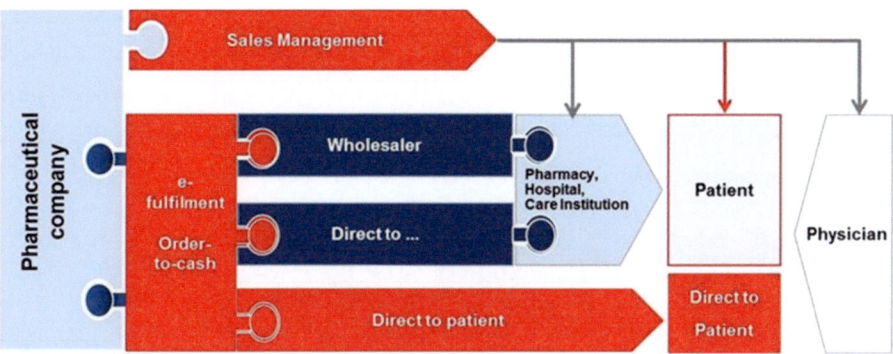

Figure 5: Distribution model of the pharmaceutical industry.[19]

In developed countries, the old distribution model is a relatively simple chain consisting of pharmaceutical companies, wholesalers, retailers, and, in some places, insurers. This model is undergoing a change to a more competitive system. Public and private health insurances are in favour of less expensive generics over branded drugs. More direct and efficient alternatives to traditional pharmacy dispensing options, such as the Internet and mail order (direct to patient), have been adopted. "Pharmacy consolidation and the rise of big chains such as Walgreens in the United States have enhanced the negotiating power of the drug retailers, forcing down the price of some medicines and making generics appear to be a better choice in many categories."[20] In emerging markets, financially tight consumers tend to lower-priced drugs and generics and start-up local pharmaceutical companies. Hospitals and other large purchasers, (pharmacy chains) are increasingly negotiating contracts directly with pharmaceutical companies. Globally, about 30 percent of all drugs, including 15 percent of on-patent drugs, are now purchased through this so-called tender process. This approach pushes down

---

[19] BCI (2014)
[20] S+B (2014)

prices, but also greatly affects the flow of supply chains and capacity management by driving the need for agility to deal with the fluctuating demand coursed by tenders.

The Global distribution channels can be understood as different in different trade zones, overall complex, and static and highly regulated in dedicated areas. At the same time, they are in change a have a liberalising trend due to industry disruptions. The liberalisation of the distribution channel reinforced the power of the buyer.

> ➤ From Pfizer point of view the buyer dimension shows positive circumstance. Although the buyers have, to a certain extent, negotiating leverage to make pressure on the price of products (generics) and there is a health trend in developed countries, the overall demand is increasing. Consequently the power of the buyer is low.

4.2 Bargaining power of the suppliers

A powerful supplier is trying to gain a higher profit by charging higher prices, limiting quality or services, or shifting costs to industry participants. Raw materials for drugs are extracted from natural or synthetic sources. Recently, many of the raw materials previously derived from natural sources are being produced synthetically with bio-technologically which is more economical, safer, and quicker. As raw materials we need to consider the following four major groups: animal extracts, intermediate drugs, herbal raw materials and pharmaceutical additives. As the pharmaceutical market is growing, the raw material market is going to grow as well. "The total size of animal extract industry is approximately US $ 19.6 billion, growing at a rate of 4.7% annually. The global market for herbal raw material is US $ 584.3 billion, which is estimated to reach US $ 225 trillion in the coming few years."[21] As the industry is growing we can expect an increase in raw material prices.

Pfizer is dependent from there raw material suppliers. Nevertheless there would be several substitute suppliers on the market who deliver high quality.[22] Even so, these suppliers have high switching costs due to highly differentiated technological manufacturing processes, specialised machines and core competences.

> ➤ Due to this interdependence, the power of the raw material and machinery suppliers can be stated as moderate or even low, stabile and developed.

---

[21] GHM (2014)
[22] Rf.: InPH (2014)

4.3 Threats of substitutes products

A substitute supplies same or a similar function as a product by different means. Regarding substitute products for Pfizer drugs, we need to observe the market of the protected branded drugs, generics were the patent protection is exhausted and, as seemingly unrelated businesses can have major impacts on industry profitability; we have to view alternative medicines as well.

Branded drugs are recognised as patent-protected and therefore not substitutable. Usually the threat of substitution is low and high profit margins are secured. On the other hand some Pfizer produces (incl. blockbuster: Lipidor) recently lost their patent protection and has opened the way to generics and eroding a major source of Pfizer profits.[23] Additionally the deteriorating environment for intellectual property protection in India is a cause of great concern. "Patented products portfolio continues to face challenges either by way of a draft patented products pricing policy or through issuance of unwarranted compulsory licenses, the unfair revocation of valid patents, and the denial of patentability of inventions in India."[24] This trend is creating significant uncertainty in the market, facilitates the threat through generics and negatively impacting innovation in the Pharmaceutical Industry.

Generics: A generic is a copy of an original prescription patent-protected branded drug and offer an attractive price-performance advantage compared to the original. They enter the market if the patent protection of a brand drug is expired. The price advantage of generics compared to the brand drug is enormous and the buyers cost for switching to a substitute is minimal.[25] As mention above, the lack in patent protection in some areas (India) is incurring additional pressure on profitability. Though the recent increase in prices of generics the majority still remains far below the cost of the brand-name drug and let generics incur tremendous pressure on the profitability of Pfizer.[26]

Complementary and alternative medicine (CAM) includes such practices as osteopathy, homeopathy, acupuncture, yoga, massage, herbal medicine, and meditation, and it has been increasing in popularity for many years. "In Africa, Asia and Latin America, traditional medicine plays an important role in health care. In Western markets, many of these treatments are scientifically controversial where the medical affects are unclear or the side effects relatively

---

[23] Rf.: S+B1 (2014)
[24] Pfi (2014)
[25] Rf.: GDB (2014)
[26] Rf.: BBW (2014)

strong or unforeseeable. In the largest European markets, US and Japan, alternative medicines are often used as complementary therapy to a more conventional treatment.[27] Nevertheless in 1990, a third of all Americans had used some form of CAM. By 2002, the number of people had nearly doubled and the numbers remain on the rise. Overall, there was a 14% increase in the use of CAM over the five-year period. Americans reportedly are spending $33.9 billion annually on alternative medicine protocols and products in 2007.28 While relatively new in the U.S., complementary and alternative medicine (CAM) is a fully accepted and integrated form of health care in many areas of the world and has existed since antiquity. For Americans, CAM is one of the fastest growing fields in healthcare and is more widely used today than ever before.[29] The thread through substitution from CAM attacks the generic and the branded drug business unit similarly.

> Despite the expansion of generics, the threats incurring by substitutes can be expressed as medium due to an established system, loyalty of doctors, a lack in proven alternatives to medication and the fact that Pfizer itself has his own generic business unit. However, the recently loss of patent protection of cash cow "Lipidor" and the uncertain patent protection issues in India gives a tendency to a high rating in terms of threats via substitute products.

4.4 Threats of new entrants

The threat of new entrants in an industry is related to the height of their entry barriers. If the barrier is low and the established competitors are not prepared for retaliation, the threat is high. The entry barriers are characterised by supply-side economies of scale, demand-side benefits of scale, customer switching cost, capital requirements, incumbency advantages independent of size, access to distribution channels and government policy for generics and branded drugs.

Due to the fact that Pfizer is the third largest pharma company in terms of revenue, have high experience and produce large volume we can assume that they have efficient processes, enjoy low unit costs and have good terms with their suppliers. Therefore the barrier for going into

---

[27] Rf.: Nell P./Ambos B. (2008), page 6
[28] Rf.: NHSR (2009)
[29] Rf.: Passarelli T. (2008), page 2

competition with Pfizer out of "supply-side economies of scale", "demand-side benefits of scale" and "incumbency advantages independent of size" is high.

The "customer switching cost" is closely linked to the circumstances in the distribution channels and other trends already explained and they differ in different areas of the world we face complex circumstances. We need to consider the patient, hospitals, pharmacies and doctors. On the one hand the switching cost for the end user (patients) is low. On the other site the decision is highly influenced by the established health system and their decision makers. We already mentioned the loyalty of doctors and high regulation in some regions. However there is a trend of liberalisation of the market. If we take into account that the growing potential is in the RoW market, we can summarise the "customer switching cost" and "access to distribution channels" hurdle as neutral with a tendency to low.

The "capital requirements" field must again be seen from the generic and the brand drug point of view. For generics there is a relatively low financial need to enter a competition. One would need investments to build up production and use the distribution channel. To enter the market with a patented drug seems to be impossible due to tremendous R&D costs (it cost an average of 1.3 billion $ to develop a single drug)[30], which can be sustained only by the established global players. In spite of that high burden, there were recently some new entrants in India. As the pharmaceutical market is one of the most profitable ones there are investors who provide sufficient funding for starting new pharmaceutical companies. Hence we rate that "capital requirement burden" as medium to low.

As we consider the global market we note an overall trend of liberalisation and loosing governmental constrain. All the same, there are still a number of regulations (licence) in place that hinder new entrants to enter the business. Globally there is an interested to improve worldwide health care by enhancing accessibility, distribution and affordability. The best mean to make medicine more affordable is to weaken the pharmaceutical syndicate and force pharma companies to gain there profits by increasing production volume. The overall obstacle for new entrants incurred by the seventh attribute "government policy" can be rated as medium with tendency to high. The following table will summarise and demonstrate the resulting score.

---

[30] Rf.: ifpma (2012), page 5

Barrier	Generics	Brand drug	Score	Trend
Supply-side economies of scale	High	High	High	High
Demand-side benefits of scale	Medium	High	High	High
Customer switching cost	Medium	Medium	Medium	Low
Capital requirements	Low	High	Medium	Low
Incumbency advantages indep. size	Medium	High	High	High
Access to distribution channels	Low	High	Medium	Low
Government policy	Medium	High	Medium	High
Total	**Medium**	**High**	**High**	**Medium**

Table 1: Scoring summary of barriers for entering the market for pharmaceuticals.

> The resulting barrier for new entrant in the generic business is high. The barriers to set up a company and enter the market with a branded drug are very high; the threat of new entrants via generics is medium. Therefore the overall global threat by new entrants (generics + branded drugs) is estimated as low.

4.5 Rivalry among competitors

The rivalry among competitors depends on the number and the power of the competitors, how fast the industry is growing, high of the market exit barriers and the visibility and familiarity in the market. The dimension of the competition in the pharma market is mainly the price.

Power and number of contributors in the market: Despite a number of takeovers the pharmaceutical industry is still considered highly fragmented. The top ten firms have a market share of 41,7% per 2012.[31] The companies are research-orientated, vertically integrated and perform activities (e.g. R&D, production, marketing and distribution activities) by themselves. Some of the top ten companies are not only active in the branded drug and generics market. Novartis and Johnson & Johnson, for example, also sell OTC-drugs, food products and supplements. Less companies, e.g. Sanofi aventis and AstraZeneca, concentrate only on pharmaceuticals. Nevertheless we can see a high number of companies consequently we can rate the rivalry out of the number and power of competitors as high.

Industry growth: In 1990 about 76.000 people were employed in pharmaceutical R&D (in Europe), today 115.000 people are counted.[32] Pharmaceutical companies increased invest-

---

[31] Rf.: abpi (2014)
[32] Rf.: efpin (2014), page 13

ments in R&D by a factor of four between from 1990 to 2013.[33] We face a fast growing industry; therefore the rivalry out of this attribute is low.

Market exit barriers: Due to high differentiation and high specialisation in production, high regulation requirements and the high R&D efforts, the market exit barriers are high. Therefore the rivalry can be rated as high.

Visibility and familiarity: As shown, the pharmaceutical manufacturers invest heavily in R&D. Therefore, we can assume that secrecy plays a role. Only the patent secures them the prospect of high earnings. The lack of knowledge of competitors' future products leads to a rather small rivalry for patent protected drugs but huge rivalry for generics.

Price competition: Price competition transfers profits directly from the industry to the customers and is most liable to occur if we have similar products, low switching costs of the customers and fixed costs are high and marginal costs are low, capacity must be expanded in large increments to be efficient and the product is perishable. Here we need to split our view into patent protected drugs and generics.

Patent protected drugs are the cash cows of the pharmaceutical industry. There is no direct rivalry between competitors. Price discounting on such drugs makes no sense. Therefore the strategy is not about pricing or service improvement. Market share and profit can be maintained and raised only by patents. Patents hinder competitors to sell drugs in the same therapeutic area. Patients cannot switch, because the competitor is unable to offer a similar product. Therefore companies try to gain as many patents as possible and invest in R&D. In 2012 pharmaceuticals firms invested 14.4 % of their net sales in R&D, which is far more than in any other industry.[34]

The Strategies of the competitive companies are different. Some firms try to strengthen their generics, OTC and non-pharmaceutical branch. Those branches are price-sensitive but may deliver constant and comparatively reliable revenues. One way to achieve this is to buy such divisions from competitors. Johnson & Johnson bought the "Consumer Health Care"-division from Pfizer and Novartis purchased this branch from Bristol-Myers Squibb.[35] Roche on the other hand try to succeed the other way around. They do not extend their business field; they

---

[33] Rf.: efpin (2014), page 3
[34] Rf.: efpin (2014), page 10
[35] Rf.: Nell P., Ambos B. (2008), page 14

concentrate on their core competencies, such as R&D. It is very likely that those companies reached an advantage and might be able to push R&D forward.

All companies face the risk that a promising new drug turns out to be a failure. Despite all tests, it might happen that a new medicine has unforeseen side effects and has to be withdrawn, as it happened with "Vioxx", an arthritis drug from Merck & Co. in 2004.

Companies that recognize this danger and introduce better appropriate procedural and test steps, could have a significant market advantage.

The Generics market is completely different. Manufacturers can easily copy a proven and well-known drug. It is easy for patients to switch medications with the same agent. There are no switching costs. Therefore it is important to offer the generics to a low price and to invest in marketing. Both aspects lead to a low profit margin.

Both branded drugs and generics are perishable. Because consumers do not buy drugs usually in stock or only because they are cheap, the perishability of drugs should play no role.

The following table will picture the resulting score regarding the reality among competitors. The rating for branded drugs is rated higher, because they are the main revenue generator for all pharmaceutical companies, if not the only one. As consequence of the mushrooming marked the trend can be claimed as high.

Dimension	Generics	Branded drugs	Score	Trend
Number and power of competitors	High	Low	Medium	Medium
Industry grow	High	High	High	High
Exit barriers	Medium	High	High	High
Visibility among competitors	High	Low	Medium	Low
Price competition	High	Low	Medium	Low
Total	**High**	**Low**	**Medium**	**High**

Table 2: Scoring summery of reality among competitors the market for pharmaceuticals.

4.6 Result of five force analyses

The next table exemplifies the five market forces according to Porter with a low, moderate or high rating and the resulting challenges for Pfizer.

Force	Rating	Tendency	Resulting Challenges
Power Buyers/ Customers	low	moderate	-more diversified need -serve the growing demand -complexity and different distribution channels and health system -hype of "personalised medication" and "self-care"
Power Suppliers	moderate	moderate	-increasing prices of raw materials due to growing demand
Threats of Substitute	moderate	high	-increasing popularity of generics and CAM -uncertain patent environment for branded drugs
Threats of new entrants	low	moderate	-marked attractiveness tenders new entrants -governmental and OECD endeavour to weak the pharmacy cartel structures -low customer switching costs
Rivalry Contributors	moderate	high	-cumulative competition -customer loyalty

Table 3: Pfizer five force environment and resulting challenges

5 Future profitability/attractiveness in the pharmaceutical industry

The future profitability and attractiveness can be derived from the five force environment in table 3. Since the threats are not strong, the power is little or moderate and there is a huge demand by the customers, the pharmaceutical market is very attractive and profitable. Because of this attractiveness and other fundamental changes, we can expect a rise in competition via substitutes, new entrants and established contributors in the future. To tackle the resulting challenges Pfizer need to adapt and implement the right strategies recommended in the next section.

6 The strategy of Pfizer

The next list matches the challenges out of the five force analyses from table 2 to the recommended strategic objectives for Pfizer.

Challenge	Resulting Objectives
-more diversified need -serve the growing demand -complexity and different distribution channels and health system -hype of "personalised medication" and "self-care"	-grow diversified businesses (M&A) -adapt product portfolio and issue product variants by making alliances and partnerships -prepare for production ramp up, narrow reaction time and enhance flexibility -adapt to changes in distribution channel -grow in emerging markets -support/participate "personalised medication"
-increasing prices of raw materials due to growing demand	-foster good supplier relationship -maintain long term agreements and terms and conditions (prices for raw material)
-increasing popularity of generics and CAM -uncertain patent environment for branded drugs	-further develop "generic" business unit -influence governance and overall pharmacy system to maintain patent protection -adapt and reinforce patent-protected portfolio and increase knowhow in biotechnologies by partnership and M&A with experienced competitors
-marked attractiveness tenders new entrants -governmental and OECD endeavour to weak the pharmacy cartel structures -low customer switching costs -cumulative competition -decreasing customer loyalty	-increase efficiency of R&D initiatives -increase in R&D activities -enhance marketing to improve reputation -prepare for retaliation (price war) -focus on core competencies by selling non-core businesses.

Table 4: Challenges and Pfizer's resulting strategic objectives

The objectives mainly demanding for M&A, partnerships, a more efficient production, upgrade in R&D activities and an adaptation of the product portfolio.

7 Applied business and marketing strategy in the recent years

As announced in January 2007 by its then Chairman of the Board and Chief Executive Officer, Jeff Kindler, Pfizer wanted to make a major change in its strategy for the future. The main focus was to streamline existing operations and reduce costs in order to set the framework for better long-time performance. The major actions were to lower the cost base by decreasing the headcount by more than 11,000 and by cutting layers of management, and exited operations in six manufacturing sites and two major Research & Development locations.

Building on this progress Pfizer adopted the strategy called "Our Path Forward" early in 2008. "Our Path Forward begins with our long-standing values and our purpose of working together for a healthier world. It also sets out a new mission - Applying innovative science to improve world health - and our key strategies, which are to:"[36]

- Refocus and optimize patent-protected portfolio
- Find and capitalize new opportunities for established products
- Grow in emerging markets
- Grow diversified businesses
- Install a culture of innovation and continuous improvement

Following this strategy as a whole and meeting the commitments stated for each of the five strategies was the main focus over the following years. However, later on under new Chairman and CEO, Ian C. Read, who took over after Jeff Kindler retired in late 2010, Pfizer changed its strategy and started to run the business across every market according to the following four strategic imperatives:

- Improving the performance of the innovative core
- Making the right capital allocation decisions
- Earning greater respect from society
- Creating a culture of ownership among colleagues[37]

These strategic imperatives should address research and development (R&D), productivity and create greater shareholder value.

---

[36] Rf.: PFI (2014)
[37] Rf.: PFI (2014)

To face the trend of "personalised medication", Pfizer transformed their innovative core through research collaborations. In 2013 Pfizer has expanded their collaboration with the University of California-San Francisco and Beth Israel Hospital in New York and also has strengthened their longstanding collaboration with the U.S. National Institutes of Health (NIH) through new pre-competitive partnerships.[38] Pfizer is now on the right way to having a pipeline that is both robust and sustainable, offering biomedical innovations that patients and payers will value.

7.1 Strategic changes

In 2008 Pfizer took the next step in the company's evolution by establishing smaller, costumer focused and more agile business units to enhance innovation and accountability, while drawing upon the advantages of Pfizer's scale and resources and in order to better deal with the fast changing business environment.

In order to bring more innovative medicines to more patients more quickly, Pfizer reorganized its research department in 2009 by taking a new and unique approach to biomedical research. Therefore Pfizer created two distinct research organizations, The Pharma Therapeutics Research & Development Group and The Bio Therapeutics Research & Development Group. However, this two division's structure was changed to a new model in 2010 when Pfizer announced a diversified R&D platform, the Pfizer Worldwide Research and Development, supporting excellence in small molecules, large molecules and vaccine research and development.

In 2014 Pfizer changed the operating structure, in order to sharpen the focus on maximizing growth, to three global commercial businesses. The Global Innovative Pharmaceutical business, the Global Established Pharmaceutical business and the Vaccines, Oncology and Consumer Healthcare business. This new commercial structure recognizes the essential global nature of each business, reflects the way Pfizer competes in markets around the world, and is designed to help realize the company's full potential for creating greater shareholder value.[39]

---

[38] Rf.: Pfi-Fi Re Le CEO (2013)
[39] Rf.: FPWU (2014)

7.2 Strategic sales, M&A, partnerships and alliances

Pfizer's most notable strategic sales in recent years were the sale of the Nutrition business to Nestlé for $11.85 billion in 2012 and the sale of almost 20% of Zoetis, the animal health business, through an IPO in 2013 that generated approximately $17.3 billion in after-tax value. Both of these sales provided significant value for the shareholders.[40]

On October 15th 2009 Pfizer acquired Wyeth, then the fifth largest pharmaceutical company in America, for $68 billion. The aims for the acquisition were, among others, to be uniquely positioned and to be one of the most diversified companies in the health care industry, to lead in nearly every dimension of biopharmaceuticals and to lead in almost all of the world's major markets. Thanks to the acquisition of Wyeth, Pfizer was also able to significantly advance and accelerate each of its "Our Path Forward"-strategies.

Over the course of the years Pfizer remained very active in striking partnerships and alliances and made some other smaller merger and acquisitions in order to further diversify the product portfolio and to enlarge the geographic reach especially to emerging markets. Of course none of those smaller moves had such an impact on the company's performance as the addition of Wyeth back in 2009.

In 2014 Pfizer almost made the biggest acquisition of all time in the pharmaceutical industry, when they wanted to take over its competitor Astra-Zeneca from the UK for $118 billion. The British company however refused the takeover bid. If this Acquisition had gone through, it would have brought Pfizer back to the top of the ranking of the biggest pharmaceutical companies.[41] A spot Pfizer lost over the last couple of years to its competitors Novartis and Johnson & Johnson, who is the branch leader now.[42]

---

[40] Rf.: PRR (2013)
[41] Rf.: PAZÜ (2014)
[42] Rf.: T10 (2014)

List of references

Porter, M. (2008): The five competitive forces that shape strategy, in: Harvard Business Review

Nell P., Ambos B. (2008): Pfizer and the Challenges of the Global Pharmaceutical Industry, Case Study of Copenhagen Business School

Passarelli, T. (2008): Complementary and Alternative Medicine in the United States, 1st Edition, New York

Baines, Donald A. (2010): Problems Facing the Pharmaceutical Industry and Approaches to Ensure Long Term Viability, Master of Science in Organizational Dynamic Theses, University of Pennsylvania

List of internet references

Pfi-Fi Re (2013): "Pfizer-Financial Report"
URL: http://www.pfizer.com/files/investors/presentations/FinancialReport2013.pdf
(10.11.2014)

OECD (2012): "Health at a Glance Europe 2012"
URL: http://www.oecd.org/els/health-systems/HealthAtAGlanceEurope2012.pdf
(10.11.2014)

Frost (2006): "Frost & Sullivan research service, Personalized Medication – Technology Trend Analysis"
URL: http://www.frost.com/prod/servlet/report-brochure.pag?id=D612-01-00-00-00
(10.11.2014)

Pfi-Fi Re (2013): "Pfizer-Financial Report Letter CEO, Continued Transformation of Our Innovative Core"
URL: http://www.pfizer.com/files/investors/financial_reports/annual_reports/2013/letter.htm
(10.11.2014)

OrgLiCh (2014): "Organic Lifestyle Choice"
URL: http://www.organiclifestylechoices.com (10.11.2014)

Statista (2014) : "Weltweiter Umsatz mit Bio-Lebensmitteln weltweit in den Jahren 1999 bis 2012 (in Milliarden US-Dollar)"
URL: http://de.statista.com/statistik/daten/studie/187590/umfrage/weltweiter-umsatz-mit-bio-lebensmitteln-seit-1999/ (10.11.2014)

PRNewswire, (2014)
URL: http://www.prnewswire.com/news-releases/self-care-medical-devices-market-expected-to-reach-usd-169-billion-globally-in-2019-transparency-market-research-239009671.html (10.11.2014)

OPEC (2013): "Health at a Glance 2013":
URL: http://www.oecd.org/els/health-systems/Health-at-a-Glance-2013.pdf (28.09.2014)

efpia (2014) "The Pharmaceutical Industry in Figures 2014":
URL: http://www.efpia.eu/uploads/Figures_2014_Final.pdf (28.09.2014)

ifpma (2012) "The Pharmaceutical Industry and Global Health Facts and Figures 2012":
URL: http://www.ifpma.org/fileadmin/content/Publication/2013/IFPMA_-_Facts_And_Figures_2012_LowResSinglePage.pdf (28.09.2014)

USNLM (2014) "US National Library of Medicine National Institutes of Health, Globalization and risks to health": URL: http://www.ncbi.nlm.nih.gov/pmc/articles/PMC1299207/ (28.09.2014)

BCI (20014) "Bock Consultants International, New challenges for pharmaceutical industry":
URL: http://cs.bciglobal.com/news_detail.asp?cat=5002&dc=12097 (28.09.2014)

S+B (2014) "strategy+business, Five Steps toward a Revitalized Pharmaceutical Supply": Chain URL: http://www.strategy-business.com/article/00094?pg=all (28.09.2014)

GHM (2014) "The medica- Global Healthcare marketplace, Pharmaceutical Raw Material":
URL: http://www.themedica.com/pharmaceutical-raw-material/ (29.09.2014)

InPh (2014) "In Pharma, Excipients, raw materials and intermediates": URL: http://www.in-pharmatechnologist.com/Product-Categories/Excipients-raw-materials-and-intermediates

BBW (2014) "Bloomberg Business Week, Surprise! Generic-Drug Prices Spike":
URL: http://www.businessweek.com/articles/2013-12-12/generic-drug-prices-spike-in-pharmaceutical-market-surprise (29.09.2014)

S+B1 (2014) "strategy+business, Big Pharma's Uncertain Future":
URL: http://www.strategy-business.com/article/00095 (29.09.2014)

GDB (2014) "Generic Drug Database with Price Details":
URL: http://www.medindia.net/drug-price/index.asp?alpha=l (30.09.2014)

Pfi (2014) "Annual Report 2012-13 Pfizer India":
URL: http://www.pfizerindia.com/enewswebsite/investor/financial_results.aspx (30.09.2014)

NHSR (2009) "National Health Statistc Report 2009":
URL: http://www.cdc.gov/NCHS/data/nhsr/nhsr018.pdf (31.09.2014)

PFI (2014) "Annual Report 2007":
URL: http://www.pfizer.com/files/annualreport/2007/annual/review2007.pdf (22.10.2014)

PFR (2013) "Pfizer Financial Reports":
URL: http://www.pfizer.com/investors/financial_reports/financial_reports (23.10.2014)

PAZÜ (2014) "Pfizer sagt Astra-Zeneca-Übernahme ab – vorerst"
URL: http://www.handelsblatt.com/unternehmen/industrie/pharma-branche-pfizer-sagt-astra-zeneca-uebernahme-ab-vorerst/9952676.html (23.10.2014)

T10 (2014) „Die Top 10 der größten Pharmahersteller"
URL: http://www.gevestor.de/details/die-top-10-der-groessten-pharmahersteller-718334.html (23.10.2014)

FPWU (2014) "Führende Pharmaunternehmen weltweit nach Umsatz im Jahr 2013"
URL: http://de.statista.com/statistik/daten/studie/246872/umfrage/-umsatzstaerkste-pharmaunternehmen-weltweit/ (23.10.2014)